Talking with Children and Young People about Death and Dying

A Workbook

Mary Turner

Illustrated by Bob Thomas

Jessica Kingsley Publishers
London and Philadelphia

The right of Mary Turner to be identified as author of this work has been asserted by her in accordance with the Copyright, Designs and Patents Act 1988.
First published in the United Kingdom in 1998 by
Jessica Kingsley Publishers Ltd
116 Pentonville Road
London N1 9JB, England
and
1900 Frost Road, Suite 101
Bristol, PA 19007, U S A
Copyright © 1998 Mary Turner
Illustrations copyright © 1998 Bob Thomas

Library of Congress Cataloging in Publication Data
A CIP catalogue record for this book is available from the Library of Congress

British Library Cataloguing in Publication Data
A CIP catalogue record for this book is available from the British Library

Turner, Mary
Talking with children and young people about death and dying: a workbook
1.Bereavement in children 2.Children and death – Psychological aspects
I.Title II.Thomas, Bob
155.9'37'083

ISBN 1 85302 563 1

Printed and Bound in Great Britain by
Athenaeum Press, Gateshead, Tyne and Wear

CONTENTS

PART ONE: For the Helper

Please Note Before Reading 9

Introduction 11

How To Use This Workbook 16

Things to Consider Before You Begin 19

Useful References 20

PART TWO: Workbook

Introduction 23

Dying and Death 27

Saying Goodbye, and Thinking about Funerals 60

Talking about Someone Who Has Died 80

Thoughts and Feelings 91

Fears and Worries 104

Dreams and Nightmares 117

Friends, Family, and School 131

Remembering 148

Going On 155

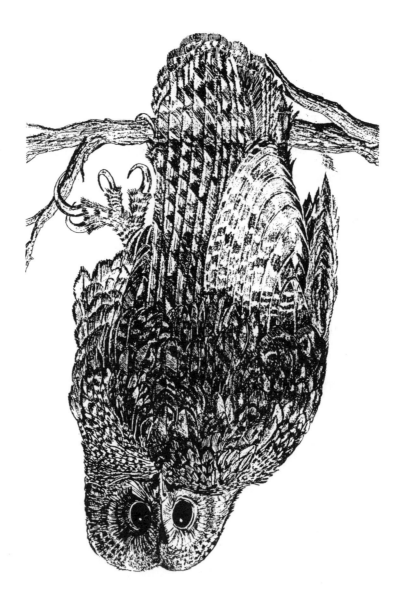

PART ONE

For the Helper

Please Note Before Reading

This workbook is designed for adults to read selectively with children and young people. Do not give it in its entirety to a young person to read alone. Adults should read part one thoroughly before proceeding.

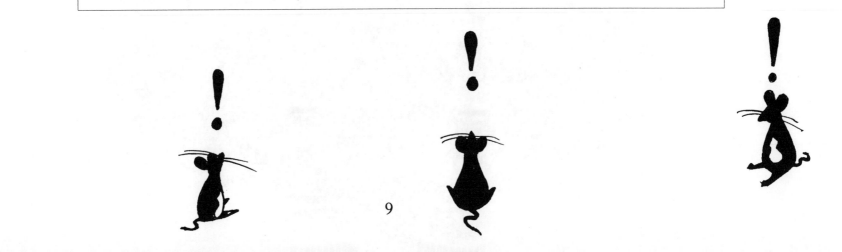

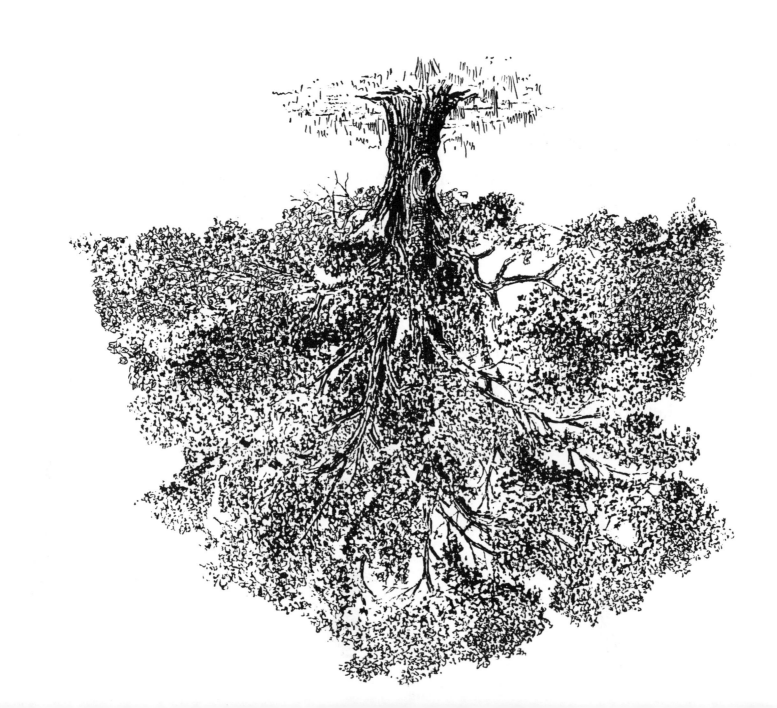

Introduction

This workbook is designed to help adults (be they family, friends, professional helpers, or others) to communicate with children and young people on the subjects of death and dying, and to help them to express their thoughts and feelings, fears and questions. It is not intended to replace the role of textbooks; references are provided to complement these pages. Some of the references contain comprehensive lists of books that can be given or read to children.

It is well documented by contemporary experts in the field of childhood grief, especially by Dr Dora Black, that strong and sympathetic adult assistance to a grief-stricken child has very significant immediate positive results, and may well help prevent serious mental health problems in adulthood.

Those of us trying to help grieving children need to develop an ability to combine the qualities of 'Peter, the rock' with the qualities of Peter Pan, by harnessing our inner childlike qualities to the adult ability to provide safety and stability.

This workbook is suitable to be adapted for use with young people of any age, and can be modified to meet individual needs according to beliefs and cultural backgrounds. The material is not intended to be given to children and young people to read alone, and it is not designed to be used necessarily in its entirety with any one child. No two children's needs will be exactly the same. Therefore this is a resource for helpers to use selectively. Pages may need to be created to replace or supplement some of this material, as appropriate to the child/ren you are helping.

Following this introduction, you will find guidelines on how you might use the workbook. Also offered are some points for consideration before you begin to work with a child. **It is very important that you read these pages before going any further.**

The workbook pages for direct work with the young person are contained in Part Two. Subjects for facilitated discussion are listed on the contents page at the front of the workbook.

The pain of bereavement for a child or young person is often compounded by the nature of the relationship had with the person who has died, the circumstances of the death, and by practical worries about the present and the future. Other deeply troubling fears and worries may be based on both rational and irrational questions and thoughts. An opportunity is provided to air these concerns. It is recognised that many fears can be exacerbated by television programmes, videos and films;  material is included to enable expression of problems arising from this. The needs of the young person both at home and at school are taken into account.

I have discovered the need for this workbook through my own work with grieving young people and their families. All the youngsters I have met have expressed profound and often frightening fears and worries when helped to do so. These may manifest themselves in dreams, day-dreams, or behaviour. They stem from a great sense of loss and insecurity attendant upon the serious illness or death of someone close. We cannot usually put right the loss, but we can gently help a young person to express something of the inner turmoil they are experiencing; and we can help to answer questions, clarify misunderstandings, and calm many irrational fears. It is surprising how quickly a child will feel a little better, or his/her family will notice an improvement in behavioural problems, once an opportunity has been provided to spend time with someone calm and reliable who can give time and space for this work to be done. It would seem that if a fear, rational or otherwise, can be somehow acknowledged, or 'given a name', then something healing can begin to take place. A fear or worry that is well received by someone else can be diminished in the sharing.

Somehow, published material in the form of the written word can assume a particular weight of authority. I have found this to be extremely useful to bear in mind when attempting to reassure children and young people who often keep their worries private in the lonely belief that their situation, thoughts or beliefs are quite unique and intransigent. Powerful misconceptions have been eradicated from a grieving child's life by showing him/her appropriate pages from this workbook.

Talking about death and dying with children can be surprisingly straightforward. But sometimes it is hard to know how even to begin to relate to the young person, or to find words to explain or clarify. It is important that ways *are* found. This workbook should help you.

My intention is to model what I have tried and found useful, in the hope that this will facilitate and encourage helpers in their support of grieving children from any background. I can only hope that my honest attempts to grapple with these issues will encourage other helpers to amend this material, and to develop their own according to the ethnicity and belief systems of individual children and families anywhere. This is a resource to help you access your own knowledge, courage, and creativity. It is not a definitive source book; indeed perhaps were it so it would stifle new thinking and new ideas which we all need.

Both the words and the illustrations are tools for your use. The artwork has been lovingly and thoughtfully prepared by Bob. He knows about grief and bereavement too, as you will see.

Thank you to the multidisciplinary teams at St. Richard's Hospice, Worcester and at Birmingham Children's Hospital for all their useful comments, and to my nephew William Turner for his wise editing!

This workbook is prepared with love to all the children and their families who have taught, and continue to teach me.

Mary Turner
1996

15

How To Use This Workbook

This workbook is designed to be used with individual children and young people, or with groups, in a supportive setting only. It is not designed for a child to read alone.

- These pages are yours to use in whatever way, and in whatever combination, you wish: mix and match them to suit the needs of the young person you are working with (and to suit your own needs too!). Select appropriate pages according to the individual situation of each child. For example, separate pages are provided on the different ways in which we manage the disposal of the body after death.

- Photocopy pages as you wish.

- Add pages with your own, or the child's material, as you wish. You might wish to create your own special book.

- Remember to include, if necessary, additional material as appropriate for each child's cultural and religious background. These pages are a base to proceed from.

- Decide with the young person who will take care of the book as it is created. You may choose to keep some pages and destroy others. Children may appreciate your taking charge of any difficult material. Treat the material respectfully. It will need a cover.

- Don't give the young person these introductory pages. Begin with Part Two, from 'This Book Belongs To…'

- Be careful not to work automatically through every page without regard to the young person's needs. It is not helpful to overload with unsought-after information. Perhaps talking about death and dying can be compared to talking about the 'facts of life'; be sensitive to how you impart information, and mindful as to whether it is being of help.

- Once you have read through all these pages, which you are advised to do before you begin in order to give you an overview of what you might expect to crop up, you may decide you can go ahead without directly using any of them. Fine! If this workbook helps to tool you for the task ahead, it has achieved its purpose.

- Use the artwork in this workbook as a multipurpose tool. You will be amazed at how creative you can be. Much of the artwork is there to be used for free association, and to stimulate ideas and discussion. You may be serious, or you may be light hearted, according to the pace and depth of your work. It is important to balance the mood between you and the young person in order to go at a pace that can be handled emotionally. And so some of the pictures are meant to be a bit of fun, while others may lead into the stuff of nightmares and fears. Colour in the artwork if this helps slow the pace. Use Bob's ideas to get your own into action.

- Complement and supplement this work with other creative work with the young person, for example preparing a memory box, painting, modelling, dancing, and reminiscing.

- Don't be afraid to be creative. Children respond well to imaginative adults.

- Be informed. Read around on the subject. The references provided here are not only useful guidelines for this work with children, but also contain many useful suggestions for books to read with children.

- **Do not proceed without reading the next section, 'Things To Consider Before You Begin'.**

Things To Consider Before You Begin

- What networks are in place for the young person apart from yourself? Have you discussed this with those who are caring for the child? Does the system include parents, relatives, teachers and others? How can you link together in support of the child and his/her family?

- Who is the most appropriate person to talk to the child? Is it that the family need help to handle these issues themselves, or do they wish for extra help?

- Do you plan to have someone else with you and the child; might it be helpful to have another family member present, for example?

- What are the specific belief systems for this family? Do you need to liaise with anyone about this?

- What arrangements will you make about confidentiality?

- Your agreement with the young person. Can you keep to it?

- Children may well act out their distress. Grief can be manifested by us all in many ways other than talking about it. Behaviour can be affected when a child finds an adult who gives permission to get in touch with the pain. Is the support system ready for this? **Go gently.**

- How will you end? Plan carefully.

- How do you look after yourself?

- **It is very unwise to do this work without supervision. Refer on, or consult when in doubt.**

Useful References

Black, D. (1993) *Supporting Bereaved Children and Families.* Richmond: Cruse Bereavement Care.

Couldrick, A. (1988) *Grief and Bereavement; Understanding Children.* Oxford: Sobell Publications.

Couldrick, A. (1991) *When Your Mum or Dad has Cancer.* Oxford: Sobell Publications.

Wells, R. (1988) *Helping Children Cope with Grief.* London: Sheldon Press.

Dyregrov, A. (1991) *Grief in Children: A Handbook for Adults.* London: Jessica Kingsley Publishers.

Pennells, M. and Smith, S.C. (1994) *The Forgotten Mourners; Guidelines for Working with Bereaved Children.* London: Jessica Kingsley Publishers.

Pennells, M. and Smith, S.C. (1995) *Interventions with Bereaved Children.* London: Jessica Kingsley Publishers.

Gersie, A. (1991) *Storymaking in Bereavement; Dragons Fight in the Meadows.* London: Jessica Kingsley Publishers.

Jewitt, C. (1982) *Helping Children Cope with Separation and Loss.* Boston: Batsford.

Herbert, M. (1996) *Supporting Bereaved and Dying Children and their Parents.* Leicester: The British Psychological Society.

Worden, W.J. (1996) *Children and Grief: When a Parent Dies.* New York, London: Guilford Press.

Yalom, I. (1980) 'The Concept of Death in Children.' In I. Yalom, *Existential Psychotherapy* . New York: Basic Books.

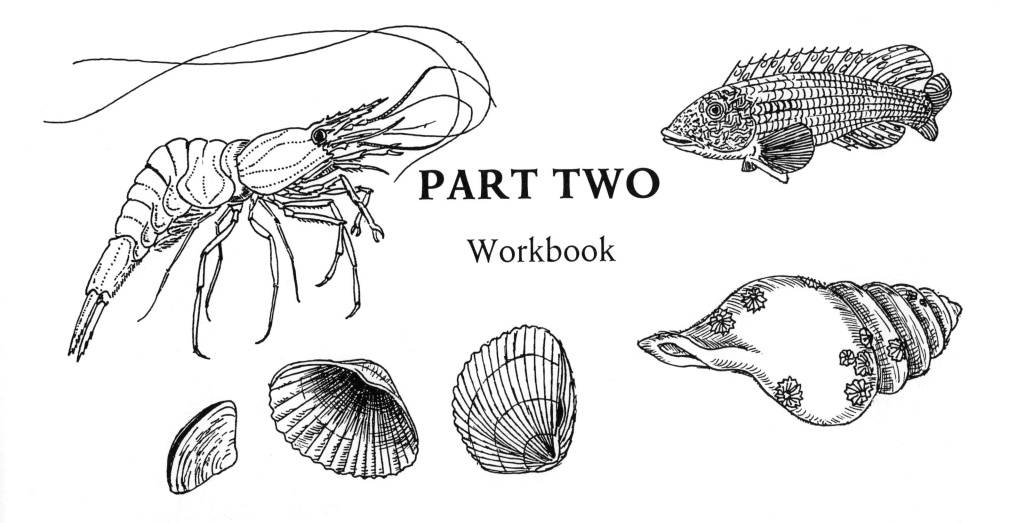

PART TWO

Workbook

This Book Belongs to:...

Introduction

Talking about dying, and about death, can be very hard.

We may have lots of questions – and sometimes fears and worries too.

It can be difficult to know whether to try to talk about how we are feeling, and what we are thinking, or whether it would be better to keep everything inside us, and not talk to anyone.

This was written for you by Mary, and the pictures were drawn for you by Bob.

They both know something about the thoughts and feelings, fears and worries you might have.

They know because they have had some of them themselves, and because Mary has also met lots of very sad children and young people.

Bob and Mary both hope that these pages will be of help to you.

We can feel a little less lonely or worried when we have talked about these things, or drawn about them.

Talking, and drawing or writing, can help because then our sadness and our worries are not so stuck inside us.

Sometimes we have questions that can be answered once we have asked them.

Perhaps the person who reads these pages with you is a good person to talk to?

Or they can help you think of someone else who you could be with as you look at these pages?

Sometimes we need to be alone.

But sometimes it can be good to share with someone else the things we are thinking, feeling, and even dreaming about.

You can use the writing in this book to help you to ask questions and talk about your worries. You can use the pictures to help you too. Colour them in if you like, or add some of your own.

Sometimes it helps to draw a question, or a worry, or a nightmare.

Some of the pages may give you ideas about what you want to talk about, and some may just be good to colour in.

DYING AND DEATH

Living and dying are part of the world we are in.

Living and dying are part of nature, and we are part of nature.

The world is a wonderful place. It is marvellous when babies are born. And it is wonderful when fresh leaves appear on the trees, or beautiful new flowers bloom.

Sometimes we are sad when summer ends and the leaves fall from the trees.

It is very sad when people and animals die.

Everything is a part of nature.

These things are part of nature:

- trees
- birds
- rain
- sun

Can **you** think of more?

Leaves die in the autumn.

Often, before they gently drift from the trees, they turn to many lovely colours.

As they fall they twist and twirl in the wind.

The leaves are flying on the wind, and floating in the air.

They dance together as they land on the ground below.

Have you noticed how very beautiful leaves are in
the autumn?

Have you noticed their special dance as they float
and flutter from the trees?

The leaves float down
from the trees on to the
earth below.

After a while they
become part of the earth
itself.

Dead leaves are very good
for the earth.

They make it a lovely
place for the little seeds
to grow in when spring
comes.

Little plants and seeds
need the earth to grow
in.

So dying and growing,
death and life, go
together.

Have you ever
been in a wood,

and seen,
and smelled,
and touched

The rich
beautiful
earth beneath
the trees?

Think in your own mind
of your own special
wood.

Your own lovely
wood. It may be
a real place you
know, or a place
you are making in
your mind.

Can you write, or
draw, what your special
wood is like?

My own special wood

Draw it here.

So, each falling leaf is a tiny part of helping
next year's trees and grass and
flowers to grow.

Death and life go together.

We are all part of this.

Sometimes when the leaves fall from the trees we burn them on bonfires.

The ash that is left after the leaves have burned is very good for the earth.

Everything that lives will die one day:

    dogs and cats

    bees and butterflies

    Mums and Dads.

Everything that is alive.

How does this make you feel?

'There is a time for every living thing
to grow and flourish and then to die.'

Ecclesiastes 3.1
The Bible

'As leaves are, so are the generations of mankind. As for the leaves, some the wind scatters on the ground, and others the budding forest puts forth when spring comes again.

So it is with mankind, one flourishes and another fades.'

Homer, *Iliad 6*

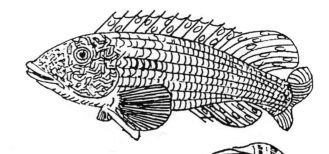

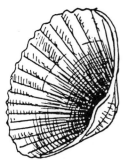

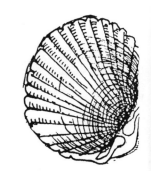

Death happens when a body is
too old, or ill, or damaged, to go on working.

Dying is when the special power of life leaves the body.

A dead person cannot come back to life on earth again.

He or she will not need a body any more.

There's an old song called *All the World's a Circle.*

It describes how every day has a beautiful sunrise, and a beautiful sunset too.

The sun goes down over the horizon, and we don't really understand where it has gone. It slips away from us, and out of sight.

There are beginnings and endings all around us.

That is the way things are.

That is the way the world is.

We cannot see where a rainbow ends.

The Bible tells us that God made the rainbows – and everything else.

He made the world, and when people die they somehow go back to Him.

He made us, and somehow we go back to Him.

'Praise be to Allah,
Who created the heavens
And the earth,
And made the darkness
And the light.'

Koran 6.1

In the Koran it says that:

'Every soul shall have a taste of death' (21, 35).

It is very sad.

We will all have times when we are very sad
because someone we know,
or a special pet,
has died.

When we are so sad we can feel very lonely.

Nearly everyone is sad sometimes because someone special, or a special pet, has died.

Or we are sad because we have lost something very precious.

When we are so sad we can feel very lonely.

What happens when people or animals die?

What do **you** think?

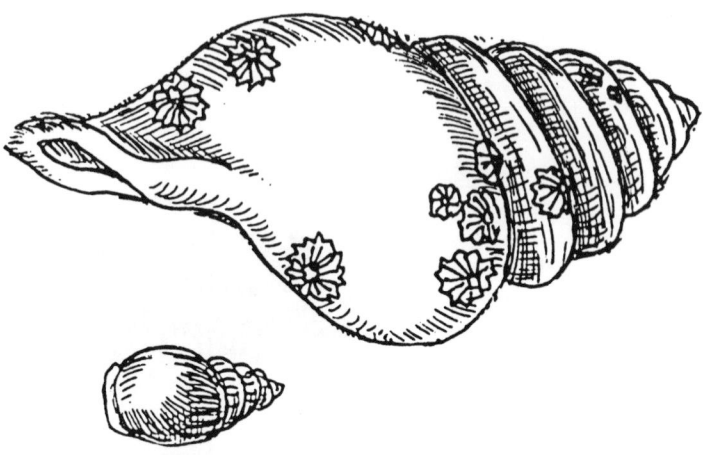

When people and animals die
they stop
breathing and they stop thinking.

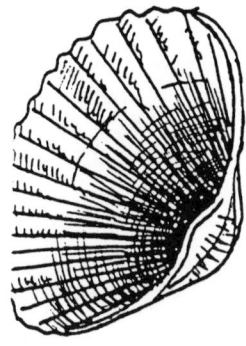

Their hearts stop beating and they
do not feel anything.

When things die, the special part we call 'life',
or 'soul', leaves the body.

It does not ever come back to the body.

Not ever.

The body is very quiet and peaceful and still.

For ever.

After a person has died, the body is
put in the earth.

The body isn't needed any more.

There is no pain, and no feelings.

So it is quite all right for the body
to be quiet and peaceful like this.

The person no longer lives in the
body after it has died.

Some people call the special power of life the 'soul' or the 'spirit'.

We do not know exactly what happens to this, because it cannot come back to earth as a human to tell us.

It is good to feel in our hearts, and know inside ourselves, that something lovely happens to the special part of the person that leaves the body when the body has died.

Perhaps it is something wonderful in the same way that caterpillars turn into butterflies, or eggs turn into little birds that can fly!

51

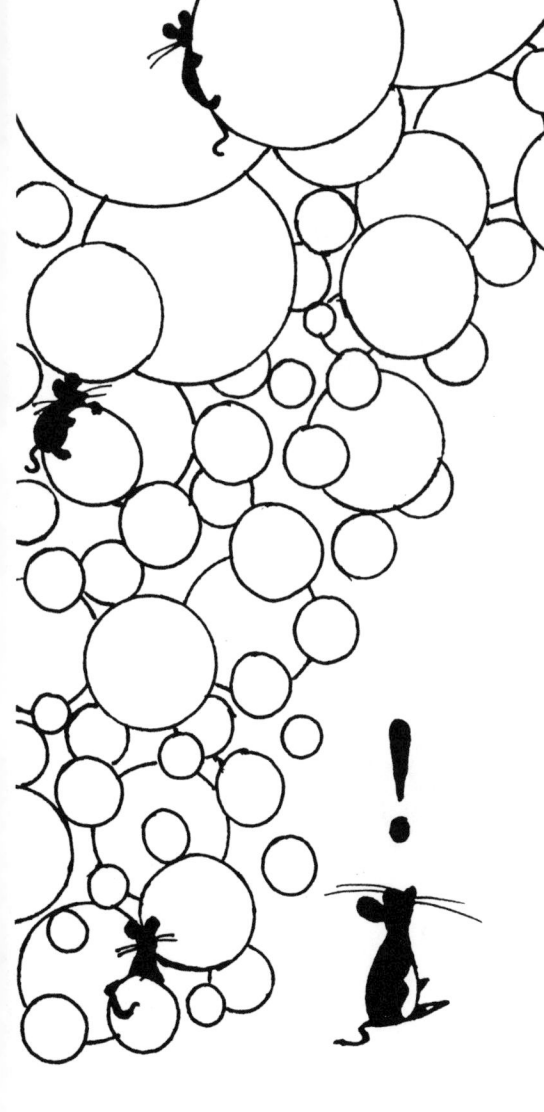

Some people are worried or afraid about what happens
to the person after they have died.

Are you worried about this too?

Would you like to ask a question,
or draw what you are thinking?

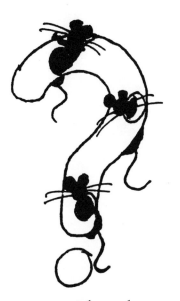

Do you have your own idea about
what happens to the special part of a
person after they have died?

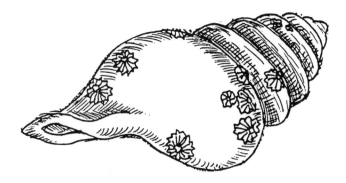

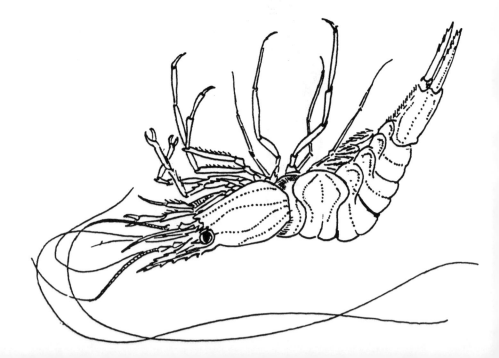

A dead person cannot come back
to life again.

Death is not like sleep.

Dying is not like sleeping.

Sleeping is part of living.

Sleeping helps us to grow, and to
feel stronger when we wake up
each day.

It is very sad, but sometimes people are killed (die) in accidents.

Sometimes bodies are damaged too much to get better,
however hard the doctors and nurses try to help.

When that happens we are often angry and sad.

Do you know anyone who has died in an accident?

Sometimes people get very ill and die.

Everyone tries very hard to help them
to get better.

But sometimes however hard everyone tries,
we cannot stop someone from dying.

It is very sad.

It can also make us feel very angry, and lots
of other things too.

Do you know anyone who has been very ill
and died?

Sometimes an illness can be inside a person's mind.

This sort of illness may make them not want to go on living any more.

Doctors and other kinds of people, and families too, try very hard to help.

But sometimes the illness cannot be made to go away and then the person feels it would be better to be dead and peaceful.

Then a person might decide to kill themselves, and this is called suicide.

We often feel that it is our fault if
someone commits suicide,
but **IT NEVER IS**.

Suicide happens when someone is ill
inside their mind in a special sort of way,
and then they decide that no one can help them.

Sometimes we worry that the
person committed suicide because of us.

If you are thinking this it would be a
good idea to talk about this.

Saying Goodbye,
and Thinking about Funerals

After someone has died we can sometimes see the dead body
so that we can say goodbye to it.

Have you seen the body of your Special Person who died?

Would you like to talk about that?

Sometimes we do not go to see the dead body to say goodbye.

There are lots of other ways that we can say goodbye later on.

After someone has died, their friends and family often come together for a special meeting.

This meeting is called a funeral.

Sometimes the dead body is there to touch or to look at if anyone wants to.

At the funeral the people say goodbye to the body that is not needed any more.

And they think about the special power of life that has left the body.

At a funeral we also talk about the person who has died, and remember how special he or she was.

It is often very sad, but we need to share these things together.

Talking together about the dead person can help us feel a little less lonely inside.

Have you been to a funeral, or been asked if you want to go?

It is OK to talk about this, and ask questions.

Do you have any questions you want to ask right now?

Before the funeral the dead
body is put inside a coffin.

A coffin is a special wooden
box.

The coffin has a lid.

Remember:
a dead body doesn't feel
anything, or think anything.

Sometimes we put things inside the coffin with the dead body.

Some people like to leave special things with the dead body.

This can be part of our saying goodbye.

Do you know anyone who has done this?

Sometimes the funeral is in a
church.

Have you been to a church funeral?

Would you like to talk about it, or
to ask any questions?

Remember what happens to the leaves?

At the end of the funeral, the dead body
is taken in the coffin to be buried.

The name for the very deep hole which
the coffin is put into is a grave.

The coffin is lowered gently
into the grave.

Later on the grave will be filled in again
with earth.

Have you seen a coffin being put in the ground (buried)?

What was this like?

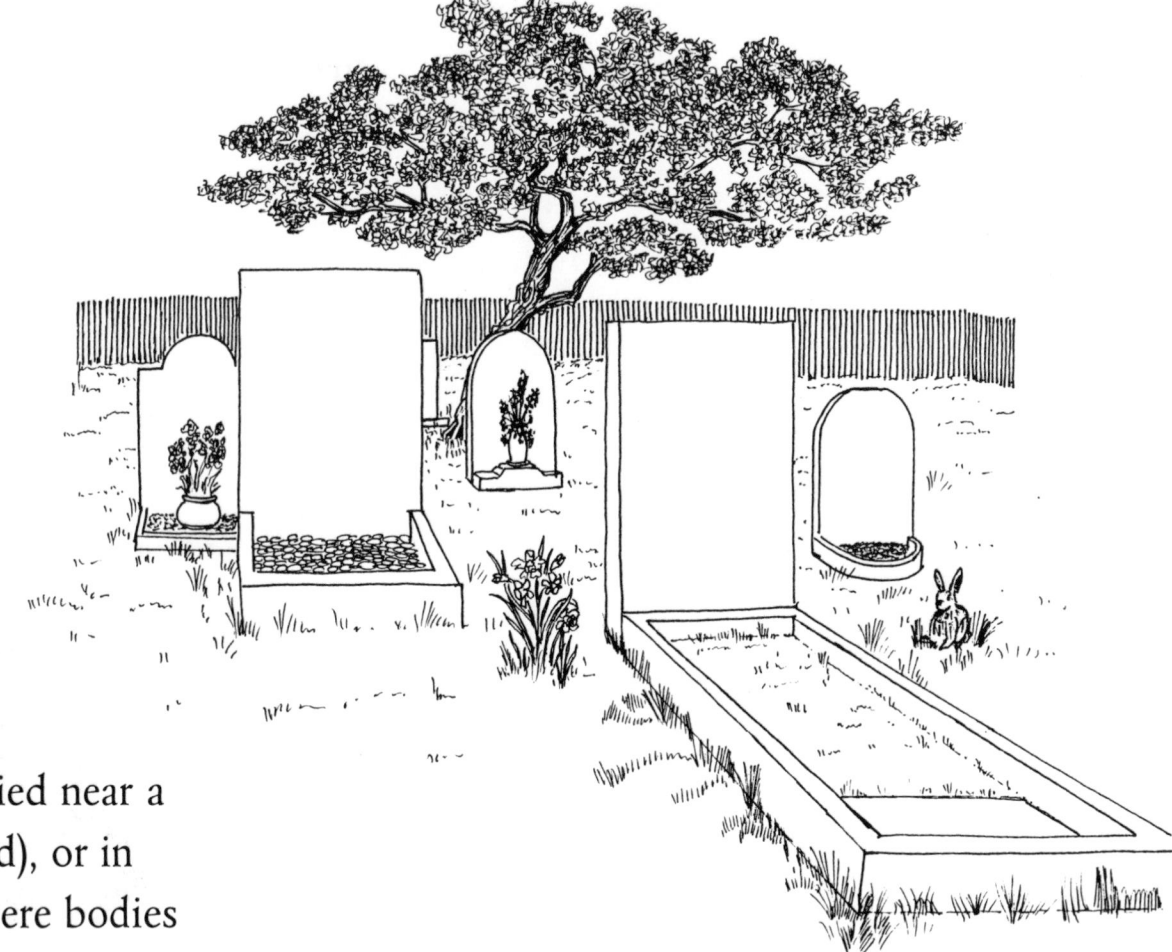

The coffin is usually buried near a
church (in the churchyard), or in
another special place where bodies
are buried.

The name for the place where bodies
are buried is a graveyard, or cemetery.

The coffin is put in the grave, and later on it is covered with earth.

The grave is usually about two metres deep.

Sometimes we put flowers on top of the grave, and later the dead person's family often put a special stone over the grave, called a headstone.

The headstone is put at the end of the grave. It usually has loving words carved on it that have been chosen by the family of the person who has died. Sometimes the dead person's date of birth and date of death are written on the headstone too.

Have you been to a graveyard, or cemetery?

What was it like?

Sometimes the funeral is at a crematorium.

Have you been to a crematorium funeral?

Is there anything you would like to say about it?

Or maybe you have some questions you would like to ask?

(There are a lot of questions on this page, aren't there!)

Remember the leaves?

Sometimes the dead body is cremated.
This means that the body is taken in the coffin
to a special place called a crematorium.

At the crematorium people meet together
to say goodbye to the dead body.
Then the body is burned (cremated)
in special very hot ovens, and turned into ash.

We do not watch this.

Remember: the dead body does not think,
or feel anymore.

After a dead body has been cremated, the ashes are put in a very special pot.
Later the ashes can be put somewhere special.
Lots of people like to scatter ashes
on the ground in a special place.

Remember the leaves?

We are all part of nature.

Do you have some questions?

Usually people
gather together to say
goodbye to the dead body of the
person who has died, and to
remember the person.

Sometimes the people meet together in a
house, and sometimes in a special place
like a mosque.

Have you been to a special meeting
to say goodbye to a person who
has died?

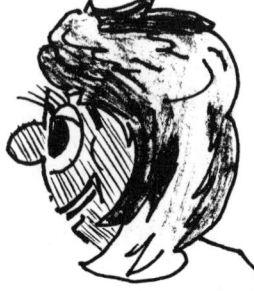

Sometimes children want to go to the funeral and sometimes they don't.

What about you?

Do you need to talk to someone about this?

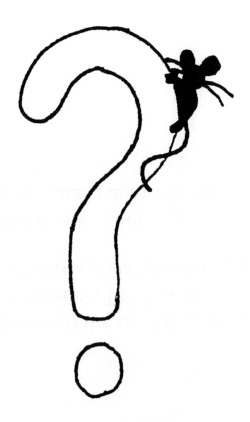

If you did not go to the special meeting to say goodbye to the person who died, you can still say your own special goodbye.

Perhaps you could talk about this with the person reading these pages with you?

Talking about Someone Who Has Died

This is Candy.

Candy was Bob's
special friend.

Candy has died.

Bob still thinks about Candy,
and talks about her a lot.

This drawing is from a
photograph of her.

Bob has the photo on his
wall at home.

Candy

81

Do you know of a pet that has died?

Or do you know anyone who has died?

What is his or her name?

Sometimes we know people who are very ill,
or who have had bad accidents?

Do you know of anyone?

What is his or her name?

It can be very
sad talking about dying.
Some children and young
people are scared too.

But it is horrid to keep your
feelings stuck inside you.

Grown-up adults often find
this hard too.

This is a difficult time
for everyone.

Sometimes we have worrying feelings,

   or thoughts,

   or questions,

   or nightmares.

They stay inside us and we don't know
whether to talk about them or not.

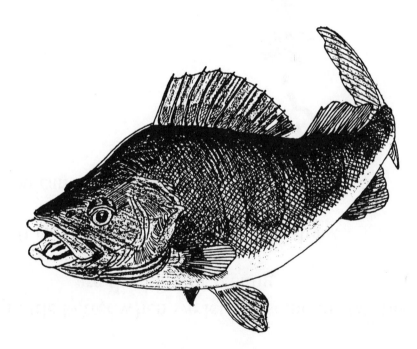

We can feel a little better when we let out some of the things we are thinking or feeling.

It can help to talk a little, or to draw.

Or you can talk and draw a lot if you want to!!!

We will not forget someone special
when they die.

They were too important.

And we need to remember,
even though sometimes it is very hard.

Do you think the person looking at this with you
could help you to talk about what happened?

Would it help you to remember
your Special Person?

Or maybe you can think of someone else who
could help you in this way?

Or maybe you talk to a favourite pet?

Mary used to talk to a favourite tree!!!

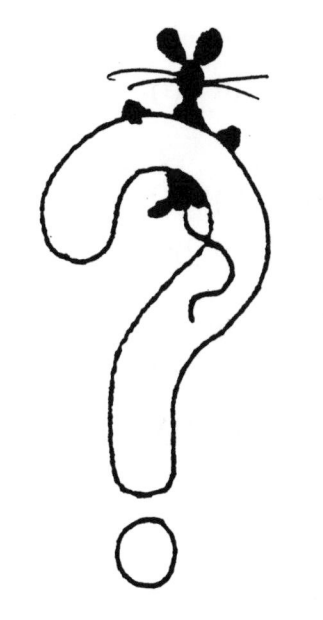

It is sometimes hard to talk about death and dying.

It can be a big help to talk about things, but only if you want to.

Shall we stop, or carry on?

Have you any questions so far?

When shall we carry on?

What would you like to do right now?
How about…

a hot drink?

a cold drink?

a game of something?

play with the cat?

have a bath?

see a friend?

have a hug?

What do **you** do to help you to feel better?

Thoughts and Feelings

  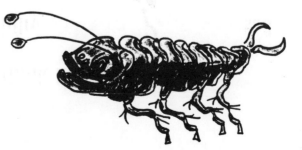 

When someone dies, we feel lots of things, and we think lots of things.

Here are some of them:

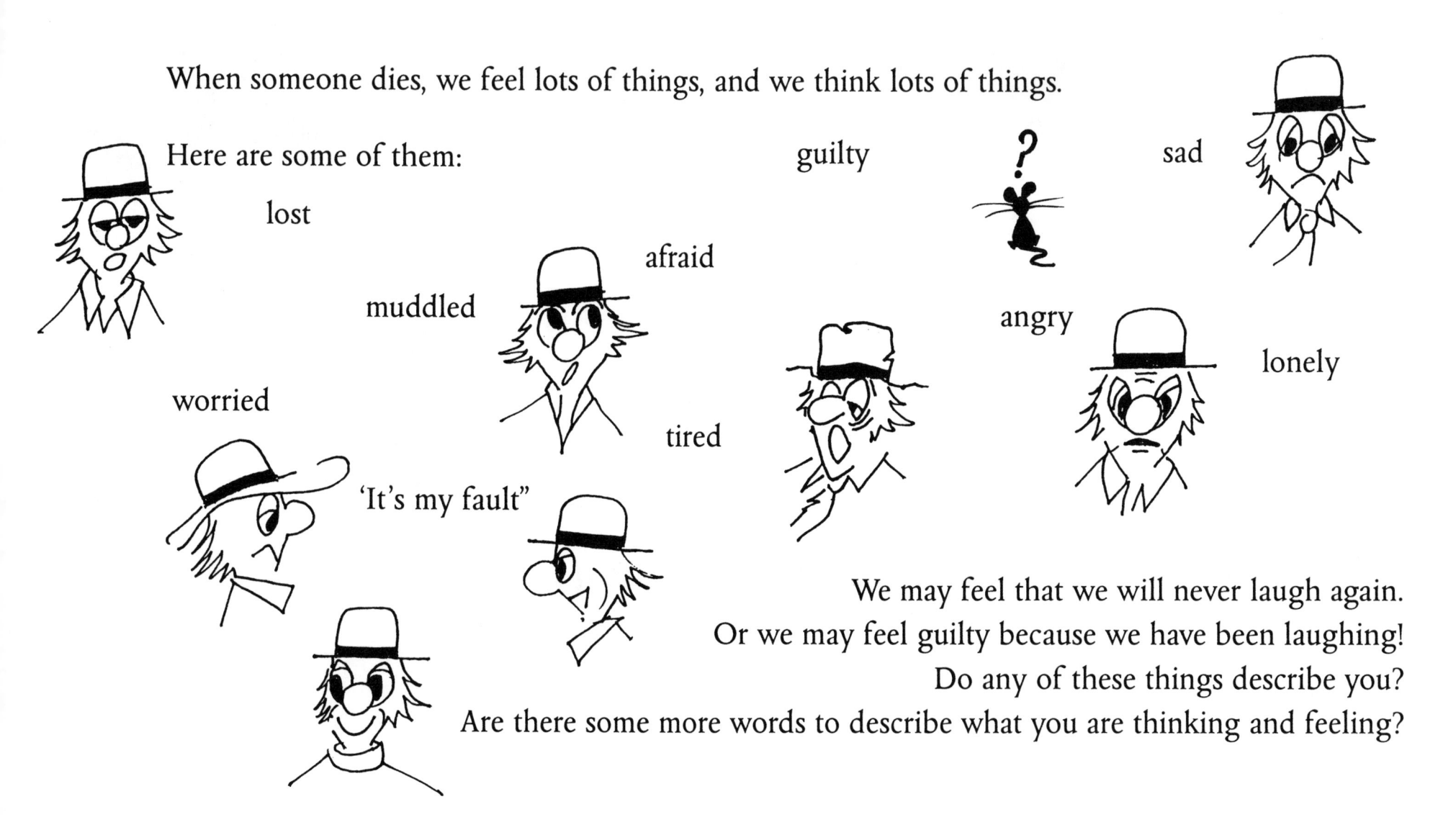

lost

guilty

sad

muddled

afraid

angry

lonely

worried

tired

'It's my fault'

We may feel that we will never laugh again.
Or we may feel guilty because we have been laughing!
Do any of these things describe you?
Are there some more words to describe what you are thinking and feeling?

I am feeling…

Write down some of your feelings.
(Or would you rather draw?)

I am thinking…

Write down some of your thoughts.
(Or would you rather draw?)

Crying can be a good thing to do.

It helps us to let our feelings out.

This is the same for us all, children
and grown-ups, boys and girls,
men and women.

So do not worry too much if you
know a grown-up who is crying.

He or she will be OK,
and so will you.

Talking and crying together may help
us all to feel less lonely.

We may feel very angry when someone dies and we are left the way we are.
Feeling angry doesn't make us bad people.

What can we do about being so angry?

Sometimes, we get worried that even just feeling angry could hurt someone – but it can't.
Often we find it difficult to tell people that we are angry.
People don't talk about anger much.

But talking (or even drawing) can help to make the anger less strong inside you.

Here is a list of things that can help when we feel
angry…maybe you have your own ideas too?

    Go for a swim.
    Go somewhere private and…SHOUT!!!!!!!
    Kick a ball.
    Talk to a friend.
    Talk to the cat (or dog, or…).

My Anger

Draw an angry picture.

Sometimes we may feel relieved, or even happy, that the person who has died cannot feel pain anymore.

It is OK to feel like that.

We may even feel glad that someone has died if they had been unkind to us in some way.

This can be very hard to talk about.

Has this happened to you?

If you know someone who is very ill, or someone who has died, you have probably felt lots of sad and worrying things.

But you must try to remember that they wouldn't want you to be sad all the time.

A lady called Joyce Grenfell, who was a famous comedienne, wrote a (serious) poem before she died, for the people she would leave behind. In it she said…

'Cry if you must, but laugh as well.'

It is OK to enjoy yourself and have fun and good times.

It is more than OK – it is important.

Something that makes me laugh or smile is…

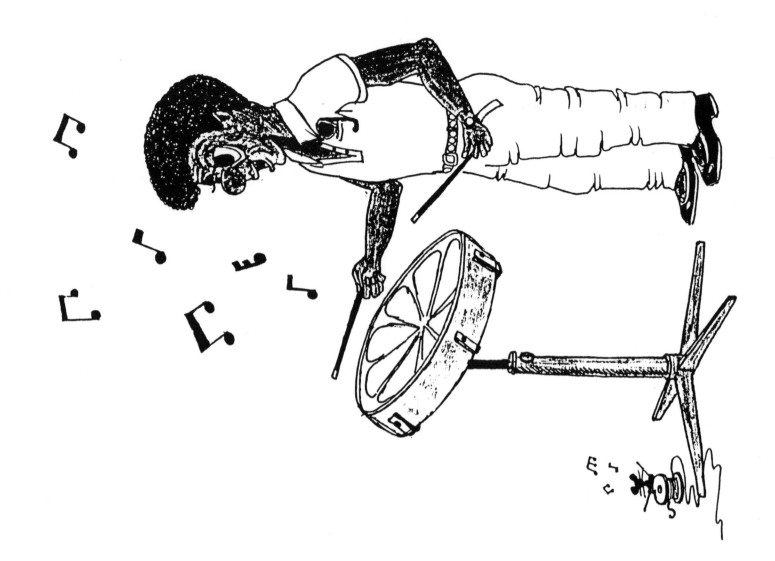

Remember!!!

- Whatever you are feeling, you are not bad…you are sad.

- Your thoughts and feelings cannot make anyone else ill, or hurt anyone.

- Your thoughts and feelings will get easier.

- Be kind to yourself!!!

- Don't blame yourself.

- Don't get cross with yourself.

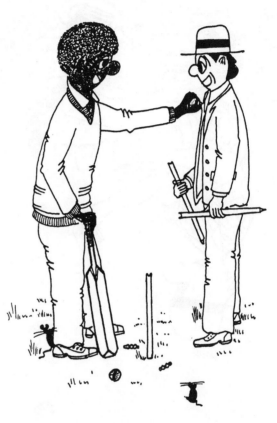

Fears And Worries

You cannot harm anyone else by talking about these things, however silly or bad or frightening they are to you.

Lots of people feel guilty (cross with themselves) when a loved person dies.

Like somehow it was their fault that the person died, or they should have done something different to stop it happening.

We cannot say or think anything to make someone die: although we watch things like that on TV sometimes.

Maybe you don't feel guilty. You don't need to.

But if you do, it helps to tell someone.

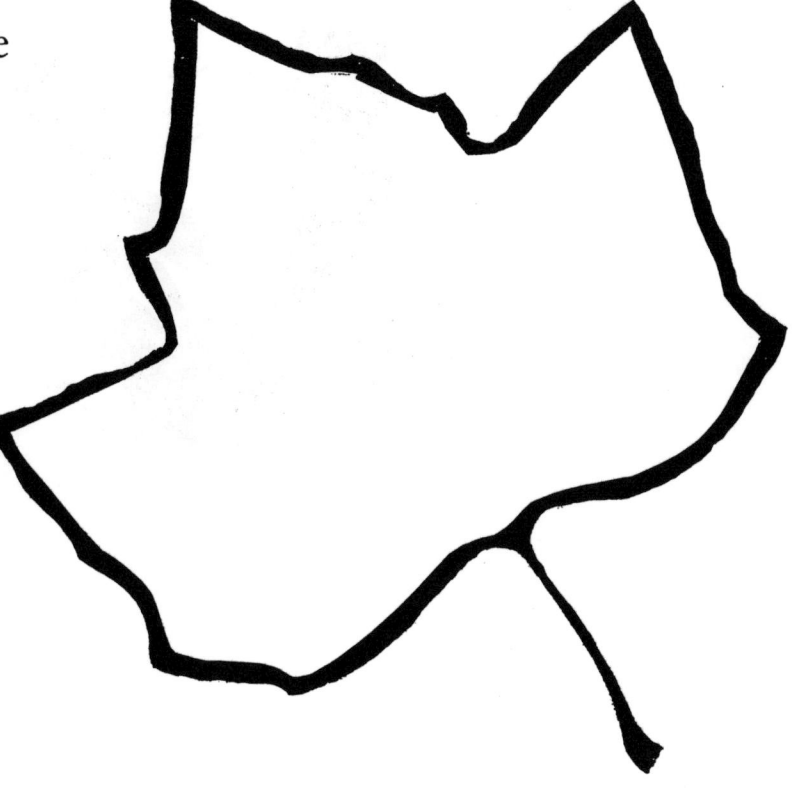

Perhaps you were naughty or bad tempered.

Perhaps you wish that you had done something,
                                    or said something,
                                    or thought something,
                                              different.

But remember!!!

NOTHING YOU SAID,

                    OR THOUGHT,

COULD MAKE SOMEONE DIE.

Is this a worry for you?

We can sometimes worry that the person who has died might be watching us to make sure we are behaving ourselves.

This is not true.

When people have died we think about them, but they are not watching us to check-up on us.

Do you have any worries like this one?

Sometimes we are afraid that we might be very ill, and die too.

Even things like coughs and colds and cuts can be a worry.

Or we might worry that someone else close to us might die.

It is OK to talk about this to someone who will be able to reassure you and answer your questions.

Sometimes there are programmes on the TV that worry us.

Or we might see a film or a video that is frightening about death.

Are there any TV programmes that have bothered you?

or films?

or videos?

It is OK to talk about this…it will help.

The things we watch,
or the things we hear people saying,
or even tales other people tell at school,
can sit inside our minds and give us all sorts of worries.

Has that happened to you?

A lot of the things we are afraid of in our
minds might be only ideas we have
got from films, or books, or TV, or
computer games.

These things are not real.

They have been made up by
people.

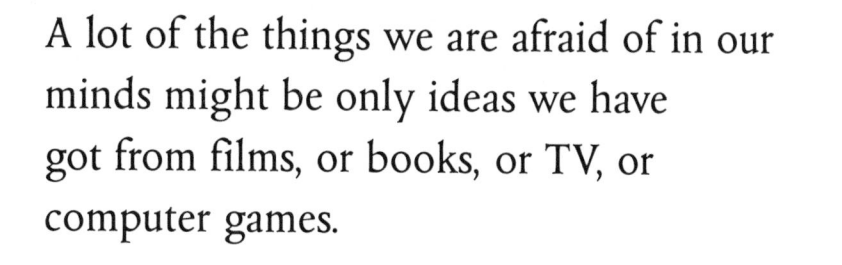

Have you got some worries
about these things?

How about drawing, or writing,
or talking about this?

Do you think that might help?

Perhaps someone can help you sort this out a bit?

You may have a big worry – and this is a **BIG** one – that whatever you are thinking can actually happen just because you think it.

So you worry that if you think sad or horrible things they will really happen because you think them...

THIS IS NOT TRUE...

but lots of children and young people have these thoughts. They just don't talk about them much.

Does this happen to you?

The person reading these pages can help you.

Talking about something, or thinking about something, cannot make it happen.

Talking about this worry can help it to go away.

113

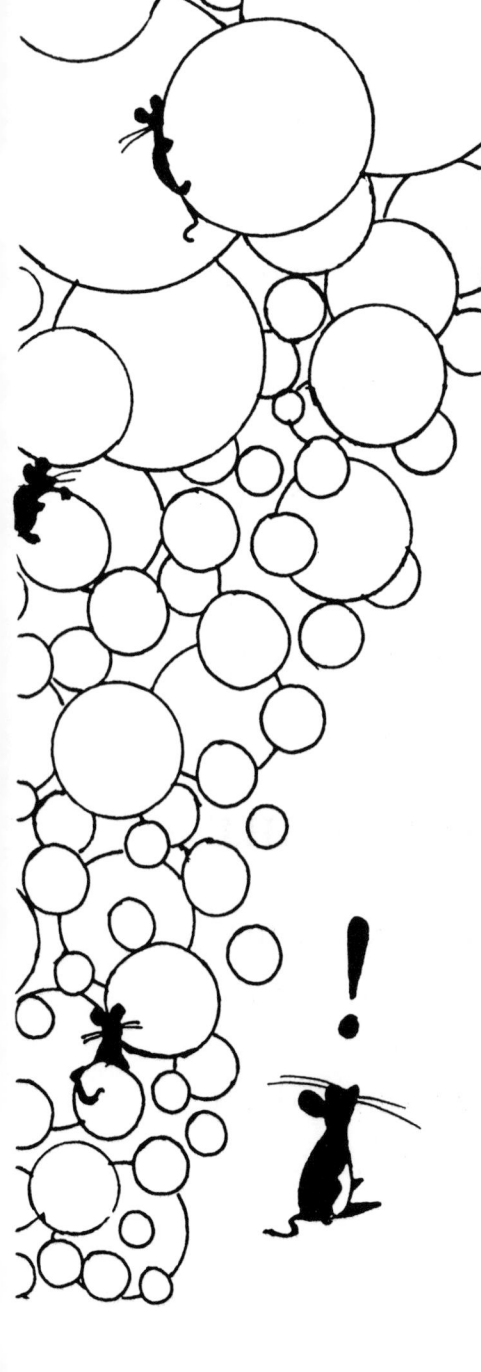

Sometimes we have a fear or a worry
that seems so horrid,
or so peculiar (odd!),
that we don't like to tell anyone.

This happens to lots of people.

Could you try to talk about this worry?

Or maybe draw it?

We can have a very secret fear or worry that we don't like to talk about.

You will probably feel a lot better if you can talk about it, or draw it.

My worst fear or worry is…

Draw or write it here.

Dreams and Nightmares

We all have good dreams,
and we all have bad dreams (nightmares).

Dreams can seem very real, and sometimes we
think about them a lot after we have woken up.

Do you ever remember your dreams?

People often dream about someone
who has died.

Do you?

Would you like to talk about these
dreams, or draw them?

Are your dreams good dreams,
or nightmares,
or both?

You cannot make a dream worse by talking about it.

Often bad dreams get less bad when we talk about them…or even draw them.

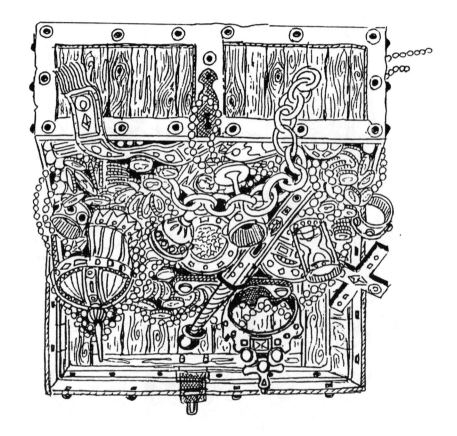

My Bad Dream

Write or draw it here.

My Good Dream

Write or draw it here.

Don't forget that sleep is good for us.

When we close our eyes and go to sleep it
is a time when our bodies grow, and get
strong, and stop being tired.

Sleeping gives us energy.

Do you like going to bed?

Or do you have worries about
going to bed, or being asleep?

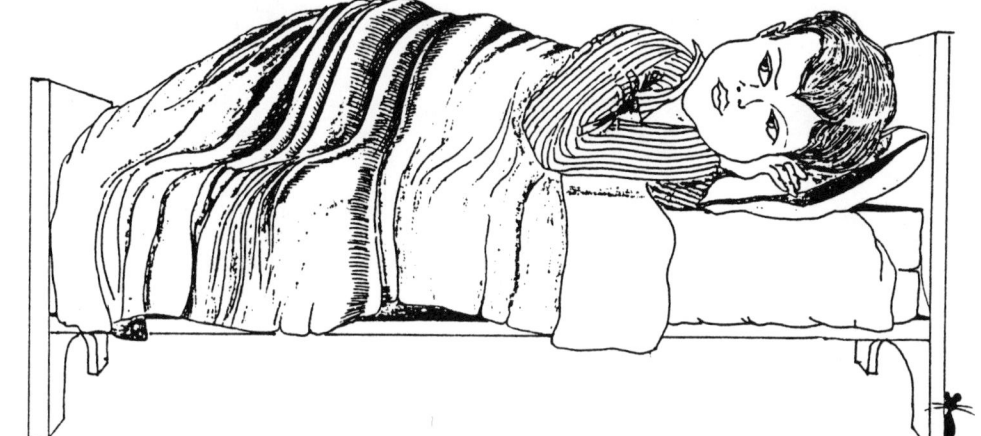

Sometimes when it is dark we get scared because things look very different and we have scary thoughts.

Or we think we see scary things, or hear strange sounds.

Does this happen to you?

It can be very good to have your favourite teddy perhaps, to cuddle with you in bed.

Some people like to have the light on.

Do you?

Is there anything you need to help you feel good about going to sleep?

Friends, Family, and School

It can be hard to talk about our problems and our fears or worries.

We can think that if we tell these things to other people who are sad too, we will make **their** worries worse.

So sometimes we keep our own troubles all shut up inside.

Can the person reading this with you help you with this?

It can be very difficult to keep all our troubles to ourselves.

You might be worrying about who is going to look after you now that your Special Person has died.

Other grown-ups, or friends, or family, will help.

Perhaps the person reading these pages with you could talk to someone about your worries?

Would this be a good idea?

If so, who would you like them to talk to?

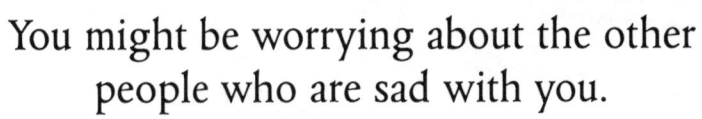

You might be worrying about the other
people who are sad with you.

You might be worrying that they will be
too sad to manage, or too tired, perhaps,
to look after you.

Do you have any worries like these?

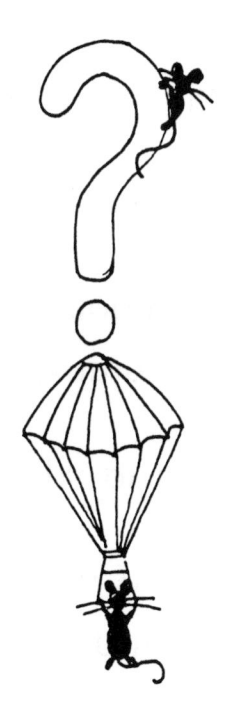

Perhaps you are afraid that because one
person has died, someone else will die too.

Lots of people worry about this if someone
has died. You can get so you are worrying
about so many things, and so many people.

Is it like that for you?

When people are very sad,
they often get tired,
and sometimes they cry a lot.

This doesn't mean that
they are going to die as well.

When people are very sad, they can
get very cross (angry).

Sometimes we feel very
angry too.

This anger is because
someone special has died.

The anger spills out all
over other people in our
family, and sometimes over
our friends too.

So people are often very bad tempered
and unreasonable when they are sad. This is
hard to cope with, but it can help to understand why
this happens. And it can help to talk about this too.

When people who are very sad get cross with us, we can think everything is our fault.

Then we can get very worried that we are always doing things wrong and making things worse.

Has this happened to you?

If it has, you are not the only person this has happened to.

And sometimes the person who died might have got cross too.

People do get cross when difficult things are happening to them.

When someone in the family dies it sometimes means that other people have to do lots more jobs.

Has this happened in your family?

Do **you** have to do lots more jobs now?

Is this OK or is it hard for you?

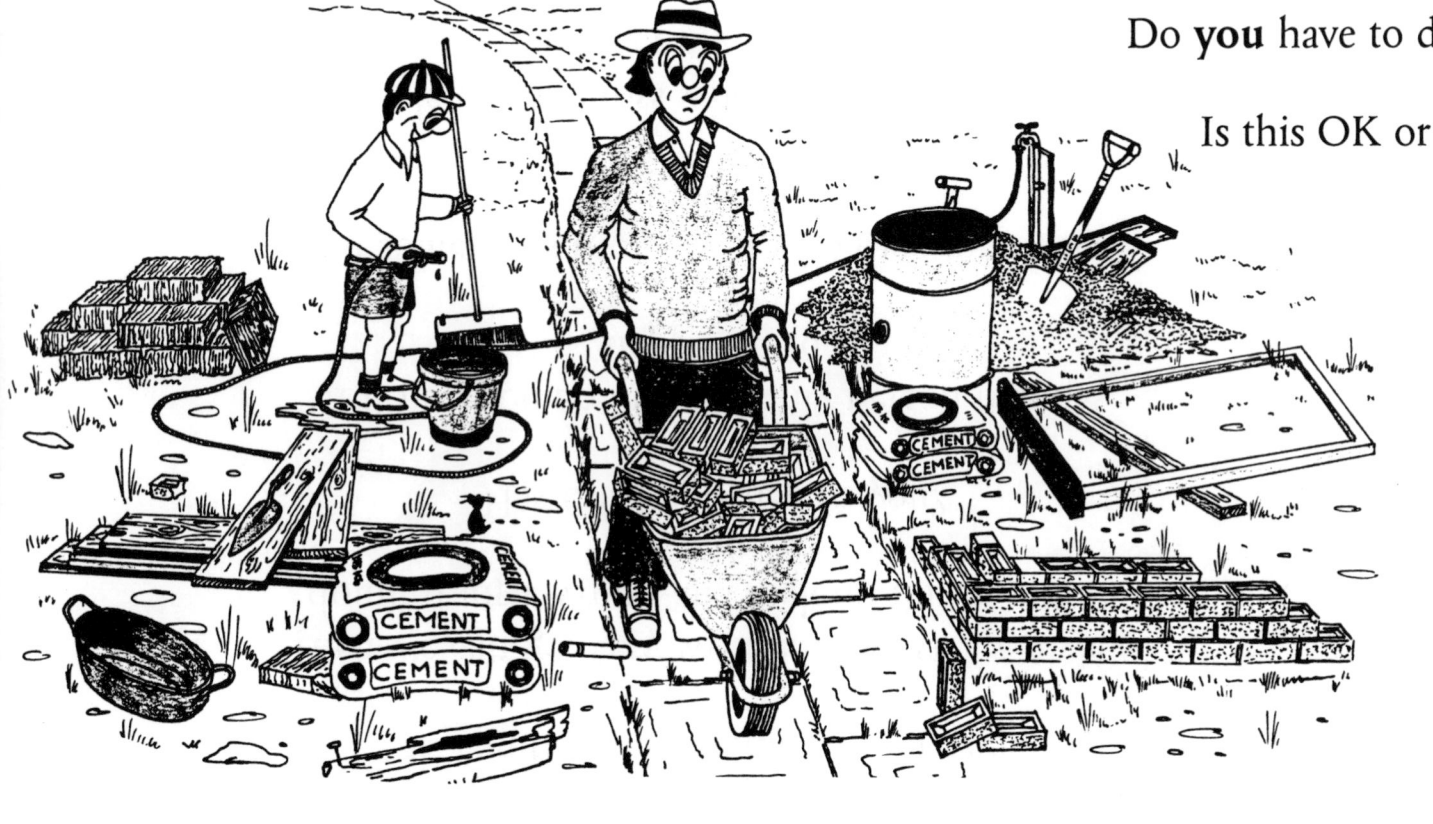

Do you talk to one another in your family
about the person who has died?

At first it may seem very hard to do this, but it is a good idea.

You can never forget the Special Person who died, and so it is
usually best to try to talk about them.

But this can be very hard to do, can't it?

Do your friends talk to you about the person who died?

Are things OK between you and your friends?

Often our friends find it very hard to know what to say to us…or even what to do.

Some people worry that their friends and other people at school or college might be talking about them behind their back.

This can be a hard problem.

Sometimes it can be useful for someone to talk to your teacher about this problem. Perhaps your Mum or Dad or someone else could help with this worry. Maybe the person reading this with you could help in some way?

Your teacher at school will be very sad
that someone special to you has died.

Teachers want to help the children and
young people in their school.

They will want to help you.

Many teachers are very pleased if we talk
to them about how we would most like to
be helped.

Then they can tell the others in your class
what seems right for you.

And they may have ideas of their own
that will be helpful for you while you are
at school.

Maybe you can think of some ways your
teacher could help you?

Lots of people find it extremely hard to think straight when something terrible has happened.

When we are sad we can sometimes go around as though we are in a thick fog, or cloud.

Then it is hard to think of anything at all.

Or our minds keep thinking of what has happened, or how sad we are. Thoughts keep coming into our minds to stop us thinking straight.

This is hard if you have lots of homework to do, or if you have to work hard in class. We can get into trouble for daydreaming, or not concentrating.

Has this happened to you?

If you have this problem it's a good idea to find someone to help you discuss this at school as soon as possible.

It is very lonely being sad at school.

And often it feels like you are the only person who has had such a terrible thing happen to them.

But there may be other sad children in your class who are feeling lonely too. Loneliness happens when we all go around keeping our sadness quietly inside us.

Can you think of anyone else you know who might be sad because of something that has happened to them?

You may not be the only person in your class feeling terrible.

It may help to talk to your teacher about how lonely, and how different, you feel at the moment.

Could someone help you to do this?

143

The playground can be a very happy, busy place.

Or the playground can be a very lonely place.

Which is it for you?

Do you like your break-times at school?

What do you do at break or in the lunch hour?

Are there particular people you like to spend time with at school?

What a lot of questions for one page!!!!

Just like being at school? (Joke.)

Sometimes at school we can find ourselves getting into trouble because we feel we want to do stupid things. Perhaps this has happened to you.

Sometimes children and young people get dared by others to do foolish or dangerous things. We might think that doing lots of wild things will help us forget our worries.

DON'T!!!

Doing dares and acting daft or wild may help people forget their worries, but it gets them into trouble, and makes a whole lot more worries.

If this is happening to you, can you talk about it?
It is important that you do.
Teachers are usually very helpful when they understand why people have got into a mess.

If these things are talked about they can be sorted out.

Things that are OK about school

Draw or write them here.

Things about school that I worry about

Draw or write them here.

Remembering

When a person dies, they leave behind memories in us of things they did,

or said,

or how they were.

And so the person who has died lives on in our memories.

The memories can be very happy ones.
Sometimes there are sad memories too.

We may want to talk about our memories,
or we may want to keep them to ourselves for a while.

It is OK to remember.

It is also OK not to talk about memories right now if you don't want to.

Some people want to talk about the Special Person who has died straight away.

Some people need to wait a while before they begin to want to talk about their memories.

Sometimes we remember
things about the person who
has died that make us sad,

or angry,

or worried.

Perhaps this person was not always very nice.

Or perhaps you have some other bad memory?

There can be good memories, and there can
be bad memories.

151

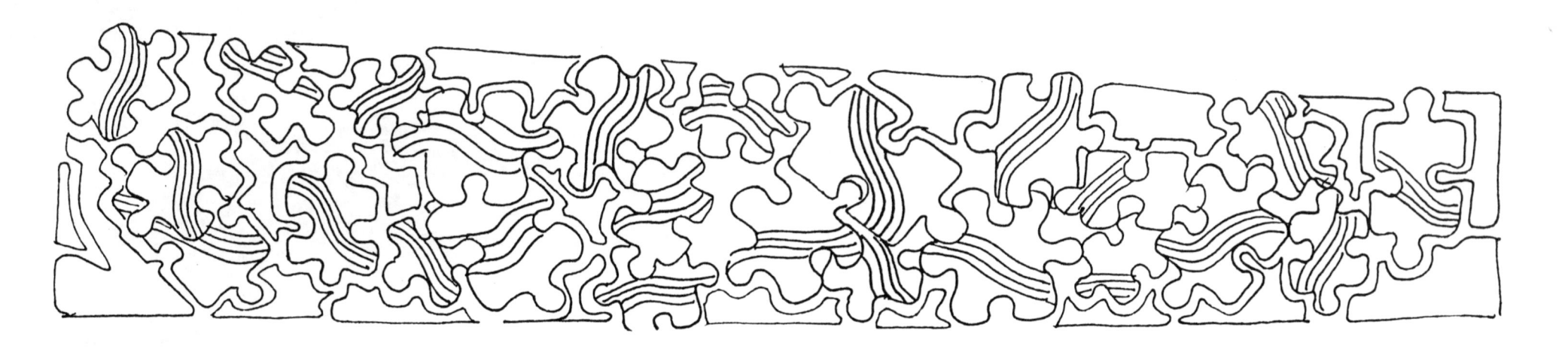

Some people worry that they can't remember what the person who has died looked like,

or sounded like,

or smelled like.

It can be dreadful to forget these things.

It happens to lots of people who are very sad.
But usually, after some weeks or so, people remember these things again.

If you are worrying that you cannot remember what your Special Person was like,
it may help you if you talk about this difficulty. But don't go trying to force yourself to remember
things. It is best to trust that memories will come back when they are ready!

If someone was very special to us, it makes sense that we need
to remember them, because they were part of us,
and we were part of them.

Remembering someone who has died is often very painful.

But it can be a lovely thing to do.

If we talk about the person
it can also help us to feel a little better.

That sounds strange, but it's true.

There are lots of ways to help us remember someone who has died.
We may want to think about this at once, or we may want to wait.
Here are some ideas; and you may be able to think of some of your own:

- Make a memory box: collect special things together that remind you of the person.

- Make a memory book with:

  photos

  letters

  poems

  pictures, etc.

- Make a tape of the person's favourite music.

- Talk to people with other memories to add to yours, or ask them to find photos, letters, or other things to add to your memory book. Or you could record them reminiscing (talking about their memories).

What else could you do?

What does 'remembering' mean to you?

Going On

Remember the leaves?

Winter can seem very long…, and very dark.

Sadness can seem very long and dark too.
But light does come back.

Happiness comes back too. Maybe not exactly the same
happiness can return; but you will know happiness again.
In the winter the seeds are resting quietly in the earth,
waiting to grow in the spring.

Winter is a time when nature rests…, and watches…
and waits. Winter is a time for being cosy.

And so, too, in your sadness there will be people to keep
you safe and warm. Spring will come.

Your Special Person will live in your memories, and help to
make you the precious person you are.

Sadness will get easier. Sunshine will come back.

My Picture of Life

Draw it here.

Spring

Everywhere there is death, there is new life.
Every spring the world changes colours from dark to light.
New things grow from the earth;
Birds begin to sing, and make their nests.
We put away our winter woollens and our Wellington boots.
There are kittens and lambs; bees and butterflies.
New grass appears.
The sun grows stronger,
While the days get longer before night time comes.

Spring brings life,
and light,
and warmth,…and
hope that, somehow, we will go on.

We will go on hoping,
And growing,
And living,
And finding new meaning and new happiness.

For You

In the darkness there is a star, or a light, or a
candle, or the moon.

In the shadow the sun is never far away.

In the dark earth are the seeds of spring.

In our fears and worries lies also
our strength to overcome them.

In our sadness and tears there can also be smiles
and laughter.

In our being lonely and lost, there can be hope,
And people to comfort us.

Go Well...

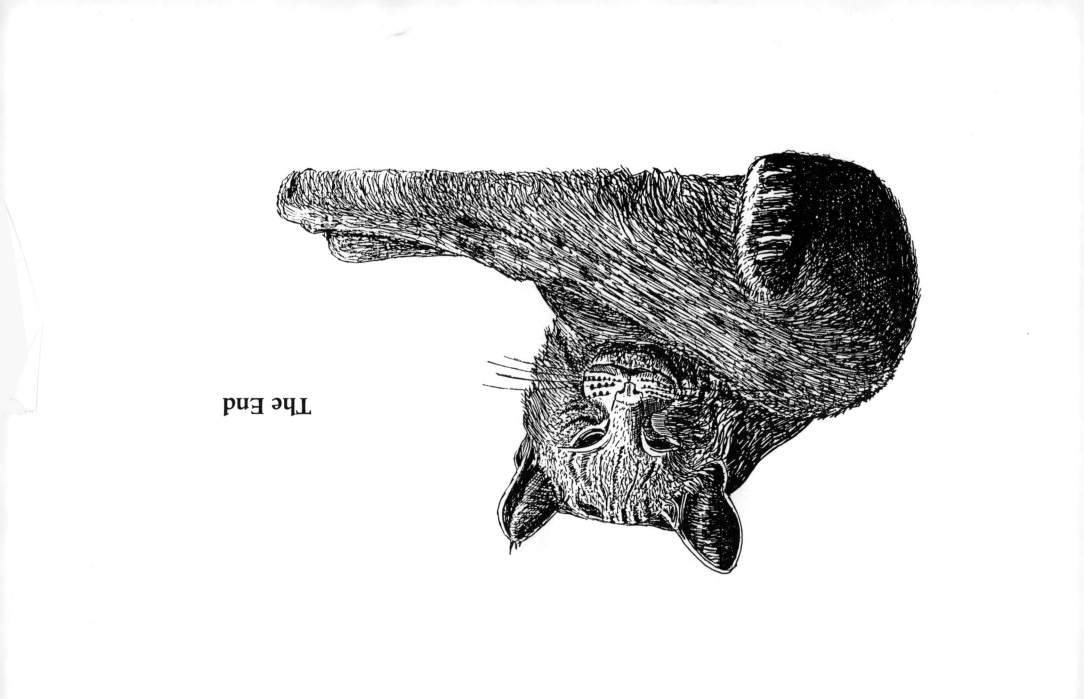

The End